"Marc Vincenz's newest b(call issued by a lyric sel[yields pieces as an answer—a feather, a skull, a tail—detail that somehow speaks more fully than a complete creature. The base coat of these poems is a voice that both issues commands to itself and observes, an imperative that stands balanced on short lines and inside compact stanzas. In this collection, animals 'burrow into subterranean airports' and a sparrow is a 'bundle / Of good intention, holds its head well.' There's a chemical reaction between language and line, musicality and image. Persuasion and wingtips coexist, along with maggots and questions. Large interactions abound, such as how the sea and sky 'catch up at the end of the day' when the 'sun says grace.' The non-human has a stockpile of agency in a world where, as Vincenz says, 'the tangible is all that counts.'"

—Alexandria Peary, Poet Laureate of New Hampshire

"To open *A Brief Conversation with Consciousness*, Vincenz's new book, is to enter a labyrinth of unforgettable landscape fragments and overheard conversations between half-familiar, sometimes spectral, interlocutors. Vincenz's command of time and place, and his gifted ear for language, spin a thread that never falters, guiding us as we move from one wonder to another 'like an effervescent/Chemical reaction or some illicit form of transport.'"

—Elizabeth T. Gray, Jr., author of *Salient*

"Marc Vincenz's itinerant and expansive imagination is at its full dazzling power in his brilliant new collection, *A Brief Conversation with Consciousness*. As befits a poet that has lived in many places these are wide roaming poems that travel the globe. However, Vincenz resists the narrative impulse expected from traveler's tales. Rather he fashions a strange *terra incognita* out of the known world as he grafts and splices the alien with the familiar. Each of the volume's sections is titled after an abandoned or abject object, such as a 'Railroad Spike' or the 'Pelvic Bone of a Weasel.' Vincenz alights on objects and their associations as poetic occasions and invitations. The book's first poem, 'Something Like Courage,' instructs us on the 'Right of the object, objectively sub- / Jective (not part of the poem's ob- / Jective, more acutely [full of rights], full / Of lights.' What follows is an acute and illuminating tour de force of elliptical language and poems that intrigue as they evade, rewarding repeated and attentive reading."

—Sally Connolly, author of
Ranches of Isolation: Transatlantic Poetry

"Like conversation overheard at a supper of the gods, Vincenz's poems take the measure of our mortal comedy. The artful dodge of the poet's lines, 'always / arriving,' plays with plenitudes of fact and matter, performing a 'winged thinking' that alights on the scattered particulars of *temps perdu*. Vincenz shows us the eccentric center of things, that which 'can't be / surrendered, even when aflame.'"

—Andrew Joron, author of *The Absolute Letter*

"In the creation of a landscape both geographically inconsistent and personally specific, Vincenz is like the young Auden (with his lead mines and feuding families among the hills) or, to turn to a poet more closely associated with Vincenz, like Ben Mazer (with his film sets from old Hollywood and his decadent wealthy families by the rolling sea). Someday, if someone writes a study about poets of geographic fantasia, Vincenz will merit some pages there."

—Robert Archambeau, author of
Poetry and Uselessness: From Coleridge to Ashbery

"I delight in experimental verse that, instead of deconstructing old-fashioned values and traditional standards of poetic quality, successfully honors them and meets their challenge, while also at the same time doing something wild. As elsewhere in the poetry of Marc Vincenz, the experiment succeeds here by the criteria of vividness and memorability."

—Philip Nikolayev, author of *Letters from Aldenderry*

A Brief Conversation with Consciousness

Marc Vincenz

Unlikely Books
www.UnlikelyStories.org
New Orleans, Louisiana

A Brief Conversation with Consciousness

Copyright © 2021 Marc Vincenz
Interior and Cover Art Copyright © 2021 Sophia Santos except collage page 118 Copyright © 2021 Marc Vincenz
Book design Copyright © 2021 Unlikely Books and Marc Vincenz
"Reflections on Marc Vincenz" page 123 Copyright © 2021 Robert Archambeau
"On the Poetics of Marc Vincenz" page 131 Copyright © 2021 Philip Nikolayev

All Rights Reserved

Paperback Fifteen Dollars US

Paperback ISBN: 979-8-9851371-0-1

Library of Congress Control Number: 2021949558

Unlikely Books
www.UnlikelyStories.org
New Orleans, Louisiana

A Brief Conversation with Consciousness

*for my dear friend Miloush,
who helped me smell the daffodils,
savor the apple trees and squash
a tick between my fingers.*

The Order in Which They Appear

Skull of a Raccoon
Something Like Courage   17
The Documents Required   19
A Modern Prometheus   21
Here's Something Totally Unexpected   23
Inedible   24
An Underpass   26
Honeybee   28
A Dozen or So   30
Stunned into Silence   32

Pelvic Bone of a Weasel
Instilled   35
Inorganic Roots on a Deserted Island   37
Evenings Spent in the Womb   39
Our Signal   40
A Few Thoughts   41
Far Out   42
Fondly So   44
All Thumbs   46
Fathoming   47
Bare Bones   48
Facial Mud Scrub   50
Sundry Habits, No.36   53
Land Under Fire After Making Love   56

Feathers of a Dead Turkey
Of Cargo   59
Savoir Faire   61
I Would Wager   62
Prelude to a Planet   63

Arrowheads	65
GDP	66
The Coalition	67
Turn of a Leaf	68

Halogen Headlamp

Intelligentsia	73
A Golden Apple	74
Morse Code	76
Limbic Spin	78
Memory from an Uneasy Armchair (or, No Feng Shui)	79
Hanging Out the Window for a Sparrow	80
Has the Curse Been Dispelled?	81
Another Paradigm	82
Styrofoam Barfly in a Bear Market	84

Bloody Tail of a Rabbit

Reading Signals Riding Surplus	87
Murmurs	88
Fallen Trees	90
Fallen Cities	92
Cliffhanger	95
Meeting of the Town Council	97
In the Micro-Life of Oxygen	98
Riverfolk	99
Civilization	101
Existence	102
Derangement / Backward	104
Meanwhile, On the Outskirts of Town	105

Railroad Spike

Cast in Steel	109
The *Saint Juliana* Rises	111
A Break in Consciousness	112

A Brief Conversation with Consciousness	115
One More for the Road	119

A Few Afterthoughts
Reflections on Marc Vincenz by Robert Archambeau	123
On the Poetics of Marc Vincenz by Philip Nikolayev	131
Acknowledgments	142
About the Author	143
Other Titles by Marc Vincenz	144
Recent Titles from Unlikely Books	146

Skull of a Raccoon

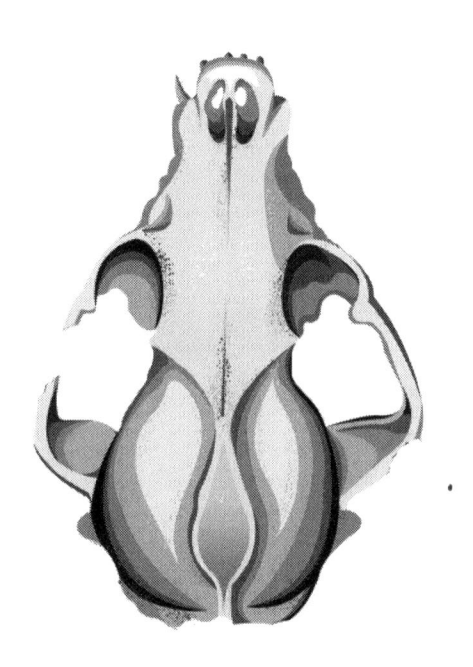

Something Like Courage

1.

Find a storm, find resolve, draw
On its raw quality; express free
From absolute objects, reserve

Absolute judgment.

2.

Right of the object, objectively sub-
Jective (not part of the poem's ob-
Jective, more acutely [full of rights], full
Of lights. Oh yes, an old man on a merry-go-round!),
Agile flight—vibrant, ringed in gold
And umber, sun-soaked like an effervescent
Chemical reaction or some illicit form of transport.

A variable species.

3.

Insects winging toward day, not taut
Or pretentious, excessively sensitive—
And, Dear Creature, stinging. (I mean no offense.)
A forever burrowing into subterranean airports.

Mostly offensive less offending.

4.

As if we had been stray bullets, or indeed,
Pieces of buckshot, as if the side-
Walk cafes and their steaming frappuccinos,
As if all the Frenchmen in the world might
Play the fiddle.

Easy to say: et cetera et cetera.

5.

Let us find a consonant without easy listening,
With a full wingspan, and to our surprise
This extremely small, slightly resistant
Sparrow—more than a tramp—a kind Chaplinesque bird,
But particularly this sparrow, a bundle
Of good intention, holds its head well.

An opening gambit.

6.

I have written several masterpieces
With several tragic actors. Let's call it
"Estimated," let's call it "unfledged."
Concerning the matter of the rereading, well
It all has to do with balance and flight,
Not the progress of science: what we want
To describe—a process of nothing—the quality
Of each thing and a recompense on canvas.

I think I've finally discovered my wings.

The Documents Required

They might as well be, since
I've no guarantee, which
Is to say, they become foam

Or froth, billows of linens,
Ruffled dust-cloth, and
With a particular kind

Of perfume—evidence, but
Not tipped for success. They
Might as well be, with

Immobile kneecaps, sand
In their eyes, the full-
Step-tango required: again,

Why a yarn rather than
The ordinary—strings
Like root systems deep

Beneath where white maggots
Thread their burrows.
It's also much a question

Of defining it. *Why no!*
The very idea discloses
The pantomime. Quite

Capable it's said. They might
As well be unanimously
Needed, persuasive yet

Difficult to deal with
For no particular reason,
No defining season, just

Gentle persuasion out of
Deference or so much
Discouragement, or something

Like spectators flourishing.
They might as well be little
Planets in the habitable zone,

Faithful witnesses of a time
when the sun herself was
A chicken's paradise.

A Modern Prometheus

There is something at work in my soul,
Which I do not understand.—Mary Shelly

There was a therapeutic plan, yet at the École
You were more affected than ceremonial.

You were lavished, comfort-seeking, only
Here-and-now, and those murmurs along

The boardwalk when you sought your arti-
Ficial sleep, diving into coral reefs,

Wreathed in garlands of seaweed. Those
Were the murmurs of old beards, homage

To the ancient world tainted by car-horns.
Yes, you shouldered the planet. Miraculous

Really! So how does one create you?
You sat there in the Piazza, by the fountain

Feeding pigeons yesterday's bread, boys
Were leapfrogging, girls hopscotching, and

You in your head with King Lear and Cordelia.
You stared skyward thinking tragedy and

Everything dissolved into smoke and ash. Trifles
Really (but not like your grandma made

With lots and lots of sherry and cherries). I know
You're thinking of providing the stimulus

Package they need. If only the canal
Were less parallel we might not talk

About fantasies; instead we obey all orders,
Our noses pressed to the plateglass.

The years, if we had any, are working against us.
Or perhaps you can die twice?

Here's Something Totally Unexpected

The heels of the gods, the giddy-
Gabby sprites—No! They're not
Allowed to disobey orders—Such topics, eh?
Almost to tears in a bathrobe
On the edge of a tub,—No! No hunting
In the marshes! Two tributaries, think two.
Memory is wearing thin. Oh to dissolve
Into scores of five-★ hotels. Cabbies
Would like that!—Hmm, to be continued …
To serve would mean to live again,
Not in the bulrushes among the toads
And the kingfisher—Just a few spots of blood.
Space stations maintain tranquil surveillance.
Good weather—Massacres less imminent.
Looking for saints among the dogs.
Will we too become obsolete words?

Inedible

The ferryboat smells of something approximating
Sulfur and crude oil. We stand on the jetty.
There's a gentle knocking as if the Earth
Were trying to hold still. Frayed plastic bags
Float in the dockyards. I can read a few:
Bonus, Max Best, Indran's Dollar Emporium,
Cash Corner, Sanigore's Choicest Cheapest.

The stones have faces here—each of them
Minor gods cemented in, observing the mess
Of foam, spill, vegetable stalks and plastic.
The skipper draws back his mouth in an uneven
Smile, a crate of small fish in his lumbering
Hands. A red snapper stares straight through us.
On a day like this, everything keeps moving,
Everything piled under a watchful eye.

At dusk, the garbagemen pick up the remains,
Living or dead, wrapped in newsprint or cell-
Ophane, in a sheen of grease, or a quiet dust

Of air.

Strangely, there's no defiant struggle, not
Even a sound. You'd expect the swell
Of angry voices, you expect the ground
To break beneath your soles, but the weight rolls
Effortlessly into larger plastic containers
Where they become the food of the future.

There's no precedence to buy and buy things
To throw into the mouth of empty space.
Someone's always dreaming of vast profits—
From the mineshafts of the Transvaal
To the sandstone quarries of the Szechuan—
Each of them digging deeper into forgetfulness.

Later, up in the mountains, the blue sea
Catches up with the night sky.

An Underpass

I wonder if on several occasions
I was met by a *Sondergeist* who
Talked to me about you, invited me
To dine in San Georgio, take cognac
Against the wall of climbing vines—
Or, as I suspected, her letters
Of credentials were clandestine.
Call me infallible, *passepartout*,
Call me imprinted, fading in a circle-
Dance reading proofs, improbable,
An escutcheon proper with time—
I am *Helvetiae*, after all, and we don't
Understand why good luck is smooth
And unobtrusive, we barely believe
A single exuberance, and yet,
We're obliged and obligés, a long-range
Goal but a syncopated music.

        Only now summer knows who contracted
        The disease. Another reign begins
        Soon, says Mister X. Hopefully we'll be
        Out by then, and the world, without
        Knowing it will be someone like us.
        Not one of the best, but better still.
        Observe the crows and the infinite
        Pleasures, absorb the past times—
        There's no magic; we're simply with-
        Drawn in the dark, feeling our hands
        And our hair, trusting that honor and
        Its pivot and its shade of sub-
        Stance—"Take no notice," the winged
        Celestial says. "Nobody's ever seen it.
        Existence is possible deep in the knees.

Even the sound of trees can be
Enlightening. Scrub the floor.
Clear the woods of all intruders."
How many bipeds does it take to make a planet?

Honeybee

La lune de miel, sugared but malted
By infinite small pleasures. An hour
Is like lightning, like a spinning

Ball in space; one that's historically
Pigeonholed. Maybe, but as far as I know,
It's a different kind of wind, so

Ephemeral—even amongst the millions
Knowing nothing of privilege, something
Quite unpronounceable but worth the trouble,

A point of light that endures.

So, you've remarked that the beacon's
Intermittent flashes are like a heart,
Right over the spaces where fish

Are trapped by the billions. My head
Is confused by all the numbers, but
From this height everything looks

Beautiful. The land is anchored to the sky,
Or perhaps the sky to the land. I know
You've a mind to roam the forest even

When we're looking into each other;
Tiny explosions ring in the ears.
"I've decided to side with the animals," you say.

And even though we're woven of secret atoms,
A new world must be less specific.

"Don't you want to play in the flowers,
Head-first through all the weathers, gnash
Your teeth to make the ultimate sugar pill?"

A Dozen or So

Electric that stream
At midnight. The fumes
Sweeter than sweet,

Even sadder than
Those multicolored
Carnival kits.

Turn toward Babel,
Open up. You're not
On distant shores.

To the side of the road,
Beyond the springs,
A sly shaft descends

Twenty feet down;
Stop. Right there.
In your tracks.

Schooled were you?
Don't you remember
When the river sank

Into the sand?
We shook, we shook
All the way to the city.

That city shining in soot,
And when the sluggish
Springtime baked off—

Honestly, you're un-
Remembering. It can't be
Surrendered, even when aflame,

It brings inlets into piers.
Seagulls pray here.
Only an interior

Sees calmly. These tales
Of errors come and go.
Evening, on the other hand,

Persists.

Stunned into Silence

A single leftover egg, abandoned, yet
Buried in a single chamber, weft

Of the thinnest paper, a single egg
Becoming, arriving on the breeze.

Laughter erupts. Whom can you trust?
Nothing or anything at all. The light darkens

As if up in smoke. Do you grasp this feeling?
To sip and sit and crumb over tired tracks?

Grasp the teaching, ask for both when
Both is one. Know you ask for both.

General strike today, labor unions clamoring
For due rights, for eyes someone has seen.

Know more than yourself, they say.
Weigh yourself for what you are;

Much more. Embrace this thinking. The
Slightest allusion is deferrable.

A winged thinking. Know the hunter
Cannot spot him, he's smaller than night.

Once we all dreamed even more from the man
Who sat still. Once a single egg, always

Heavenly, always
Arriving.

Open the window, come see the far-flung
Spring leaves, the dividing land and the
Iced air, the web of glass beads,

The shallow walls, the breathing,
The heaving of the outdoors.

Instilled

In instinct, unwavering, absorbing
That masterly recast on Corsica or
Cordoba. The passage of time is in years.

We don't go south, they say. It's too meager,
It's not what it wanted to be, it adheres
To the tides, that falling strength,

The strands that weave, that hold to us fast.
The heart thrashes, and so too, perhaps
May be defined in the Delta, where walls

Are cinnabar, and the green of trees
Stretches skyward. Those human acts
Of which we're accused, the road caked

At window level, this swarm of disappearing
Acts. All hands on deck. Do you feel
The fattening of waistlines, the city street

At your side, that going down into
The flinching just by the tavern door,
That plunging into sincerity—All those costs!

Don't you wish to fuse with the sky,
To toss the chicken bones into the sea?
Don't you wish to become the gnarled tree?

Or the breakers on the sea and the brown
Rocks in their gentle lapping. Child's play.
Ah, to change the void and all that sparring.

Pelvic Bone of a Weasel

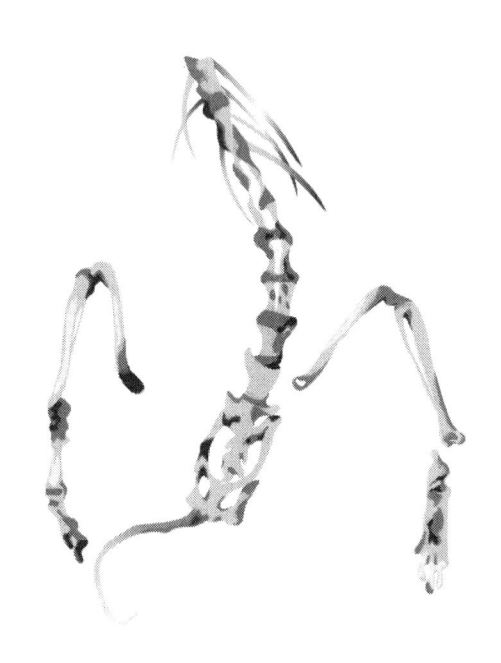

Inorganic Roots on a Deserted Island

Infernal, burst upon burst, the voices
Of blood holed up counting cash, even
As the swallows bring in wisps of grass.

9:00 a.m. The pharmacist prepares his paper-
Work while his Man Friday dreams
Of deserted islands. In the garden, acorns

Thud against the wall. Leaves spiral.
Land in the ditch. A fatherly voice
Mumbles in the sticky heat. From upon

The bridge, down to the canal below,
The sun says grace. Here you will find
The lots have been cast, and the mice

Play dice. "Be our merry guest," you say,
Your hair light as plumage almost
Beckoning the way. You pour out the wine

In that fatherly way, stare across
The canal, remembering: "Something pulls
Us toward the invisible. Just know

The rules of the game—the unracking
Of boundaries remains unspoken, of course.
Talk about hard work. That's bound to impress.

And know that tomorrow never comes."
The wine tastes light, just like your hair,
Cut with tapwater I'd hazard a guess.

"Let's wait until evening," you say,
"We don't know yet who's staying."

    And so I climb the cliffs just as you
    Suggested and inch my way toward the crux.
    Bitter blindness descends as I rise, a vapor

    Of thought swirls above my head.
    At the peak a stork leans into the sky.
    Beyond the clouds, undeviated flight.

    Everything seems so familiar, lifeless.
    I see the years welling in many faces,
    The print of land over the arch of wind.

Evenings Spent in the Womb

Who sides with whom?
Who with what passport?
Who with which percentage?

And the pleasure threefold
Before we glance at our wills.
The chronicle breaks off,

Wings are folded
And we dive into the foundations
More like a pelican than a goose.

Here solitary green algae
Screw themselves together
Becoming one, two, three!

A beetle sits in the sun.

Here we find museum catalogues,
Everything arranged in parley,
And, of course, in other modes of expression.

Who gives with whom?
Who with an unexpected event?
Who with the ill-omened?

A dream is not a season.

Our Signal

Yes, we met largely by mistake.
Probably you're no longer
What you once were.

Rough edges rubbed smooth.
You are a hieroglyph larger than life.
Your choice, you say, asking

Your own illusions. Bull's-eye.
Have you seen an instant, or
Were you deluded into thinking so?

It happens some days that being
Spiritual won't radiate
A magnetic field. Only by

Being, your magic arises.
Run toward the trees, grasp
The green shoots—seal your fate

Which brims, overflowing. If innocence
Is at fault, then I know everything
And I know nothing.

A Few Thoughts

The views from the bridges, high above the Taj Mahal, the deserts of Northern India, the shining pools and dense scrub, the rapids and the trains.

Suddenly there was a flash of light and the suitcase was crawling with insects. A small tree was at its center, and growing beside, thousands of mushrooms: chanterelles, polypores and morels, the Penny Bun and the Hen of the Woods, the Lobster and the Jack-o'-Lantern.

I wanted to climb that tree, but I was watchful.

For hours I stood there pondering the life of fungi, all wrapped up in a blanket.

So I grabbed the suitcase, shut it tight, lipped the words—a few nothings to remind me.

You see, the tangible is all that counts.

I whistled for the train.

A woman's voice said: "Saturday. Next Saturday."

Far Out

The fleeting clatter of keys.
Everyone is taking cover in dictionaries.

The moon, lost in its whereabouts
Shining through storm clouds—

Smatterings of politics, science,
Of philosophy. Maybe if someone dies

Tonight, the terrestrial gods will visit.
Above the world, mistakes take hold—

Numbering in the thousands. A hole
The size of Manhattan bleeding down

In elemental cubits. No recognition,
Simply disguises—some have called him

'He Who Shines Through the Darkness.'
[Something about dark matter here.

Not electromagnetic, and it should
Be noted that this creature is composed

Of a formless multiform and swifter
Than electrons whirling in flash lightning.]

"So where are all the feathers?" you ask.
"We do not know you as you now do," she sputters.

The compass needle wavers, travels far
Looking for a hearing. You squeeze the case,

Cradle the base like ripened fruit.
"Bear with me," she says. "Smoke smoke

Smoke. It's all smoke. The mirrors, you see,
Have been shattered long ago."

"Compassionate man," says this woman
Dreamily on a boat drifting down.

"The river knows …" she says,
"The river knows nothing of itself."

Fondly So

There's no arguing with shadows.
Surprised? Once on a flight

From Vancouver, a Venetian woman
Assured me that languages have been

Jumbled for millennia—"Several voices
Speak as once, or—at once. At least

For a second, the receiver of the con-
Versation thinks she is alive. Another

Th-thinks I'm dead," she said, stammering,
"Soon we'll have to be resigned

To half-speech. The world, of course
Is mute." I went back to that dreary

Flophouse in Shanghai, assured the pot
It was ready for boiling, but the shadows

Concealed themselves. A first refuge
Revealed the essence of their memory.

"Handcuffs!" the man said clenching
His teeth. A form of survival, I thought.

In between the applause and the ribbons
There will be something else, some-

Thing like habitat where existence
Is really possible without exaltation,

Where habitat is liberation, where
Exile and martyrdom are the best

Means safe from infamy. Jesus Christ!
To be liberated is surely to be divine.

Now we are between churches, nothing
In common but the rhyme. Absurd

All that time spent on hope. Still,
I suppose anything that exists

Beyond the existable awakens
The most profound shadows.

All Thumbs

Mushrooms like fingers
Push up through the soil.

The robins seem disinterested.

There's enough seed here
To go around.

A warm current down at the knees.

Standing in place, following
The cooked flight path

Of the corpulent bumblebees.

They're back this year
The size of thumbs.

The murmuring turkeys,
The gurgling killdeer—

And the slow mumble of traffic

Far beyond the pines.
There's still someone out there

Turning wheels

But deeply invisible.

Fathoming

There are those who advise me
To preserve these fragments.

Forgive me, but there is nothing
That walks toward us. Find

The heavenly gates, they say, but only
Once you're several pages in.

The unwritten somehow glides through.
It's very persistent, but likely

A bad bargain. Remember the hour
Of no words, the clunking of

The antique sewer system, the hatch
That opens above when night falls.

Tear yourself away from these words
Even if the letters pile up,

All questions go unanswered. Who
Would have thought so?

Bare Bones

Unlearning what came before,
Unlearning the murder on 22nd Street,
Unlearning the cast of characters,

The where the when the how the why
Until the Dow Jones took off again,
And still the grave has a bunch of posies,

And your shoelaces creak as you reach
To put them in place, even when
They are Hangzhou silk and Ningbo plastic.

Unwondering what came before.
Unwondering that curve on the horizon,
Unwondering the thief who snatched your purse

On some unknown avenue in Sao Paolo.
Did we truly cross an unfamiliar threshold?
Unlearn all those lessons in the woods?

We leapt hard and high on our foolhardy feet,
This was the gin the gods mixed in their martinis.
This was the last dance exiting alone.

A real high-on-the-nite job!
And even when she turns to sigh,
The grass is still sprinkled with gold.

And we move on to a major highway
Knowing it's better for our health.
Can a man like me bounce back?

You know it's all in the wrist, but
As Jaroslav once said, "The others
Are simply apparitions, they are creatures

Of another purpose. The defect is in
The boat. Drop your eyes. Who can twist
The counterforce, force open the iron gates

Of the keep? Atone alone, Dear Creature.
Truth matters. Even the Mithraists
Cultivated a mystique. The Renaissance was no

Romance, believe me. And yes, they had
An armistice, and yes, Italy is not in
Our hearts but in our bones.

Common law suggests is all not lost yet."

Facial Mud Scrub

On a calm day the sun seeks sweet wildflowers.
Each soul is alone, no consolation in crowds.

As the railway sleeks northward, lovers are in despair
Waiting for that fateful moment of self-discovery.

Too young to atone for the sins of the fathers,
Too old to care—life is hard enough, even no consolation.

≈

On that night a star vanished, simply ignited in a ball
of contemplation, an afterthought
                        of drizzle quenching the herbage.

Draped in our towels, we do atone for the ill deeds
And deathly nights before enlightenment, to read

The sum of things, those who didn't make it
Or made it through the middle drains down in the parish.

≈

Lightning in the summer sky upon the meadow and vale.
More a streaming than a breath, then in another way, not

Satisfying; even with all our ointments and our lathers,
Muds of varying colors, the peacock strutting beneath

That glassy dome, and in the center the fountain spouting,
A languid amphibian rises squirting scents to inhibit

≈

And surprise, to seduce, to vandalize; in everything
A sense of excretion, of exorcism, of transmogrification,

A known deed, the foundations
           of folly and deep exercise—
And the cheese un-holed, clenched tight as a lactose-

Intolerant fist, streaked in a pottage of dill and thyme,
But thin, spaced out in fingerbowls with crackers made

≈

Of rice. No hesitation though, the eradication faintly wry
Or condescending, might be the last surprise seen.

And yet, here we dwell on the remainder of a forest
On the edge of the last stripmall where lounging seniors

Fly to the outer limits, where everyone is kept on
A bright red, bejeweled leash. Sparkling in food lamps

≈

They wave at you on the way to the door, and in your head
Those two lines about love too wild to repeat here.

Oh, and in these happy moments of dread and delight,
Through the turnstile across the hall, deep down

In the keep, that keepsake temple where trinkets
Are passed around,
          where all that gnawing and nibbling goes on;

≈

The mold lining the casements, the climate just vent-
Ilated enough to connote an ample wild breeze.

Oh for the love of the ample, the efficient sufficient,
The doorframe that makes you bend your head,

Vowed to measure and trace, to live for the liver
And the lungs, to the Our-Fathers-Still-to-Come,

≈

To dwell on the edge of absolution and write only
Of one simple dream—a luxury, or perhaps something

More sinister … Passion-pink toenails are all the rage;
Or perhaps something like winning the Nobel Prize

In abject apathy, to stride forth with nothing in the back
Of your head, but to revert back to birth—peach-

≈

Blossom-skinned, luxuriant, smelling of goose feathers.

From our bathroom door, the light sneaks in,

Measured sounds of laughter and clapping. Honestly,
It's rough to begin again—
whose eyes should you seek first?

Whose hair to ply or multiply? Even as we speak
several dots appear on the horizon.

Sundry Habits, No.36

The dimensions of

Your rational be-
Havior, long ago,

In the stream of
Time; the sparks

Of our forebears'
Souls, time was

Swift, never par-
Ticular, somewhat

Mockingly nudging
Us forward like

Ectoplasm.　　　　　We all

Wanted the same,
Even in the man-

Groves of Saloum,

Over the crags of
Peru and their high-
flying
Strands of cloud-
Cover.

                        Watch how
The blackbird lays
Her eggs—simple,

Delicate, without
Fuss—the queen

Has yet to be born—

In these dimensions
                        The future is not

Yet written. Fold
Your umbrellas,
Avoid the pedantic

Commentary, defer to
The seabirds, in their
Total projected ass-

Ault, their ruffle on
The wings of time.
                        The storm

Rides in the catamaran,
Dangerous faults deep

In the earth's crust—
Evidence accumulates.
It's neither now
Nor never, ether or

Fire. Those few
Magnolia buds worked
Their way through

The rubble, counted
Each broken stone,

In that house
On Mulberry Street.

Land Under Fire After Making Love

These seven deadly sins; the lights,
By the way, were red, and even as the night
Surrendered and regret resurfaced, you wore

Your crown well—tilted, at a gentle 15 degrees,
And that photo of you at the statue
Of Venus—Oh! The Lights! Impeccable!

The memory reaches back, a droplet of sweat
On your temple, that bewitching glitter,
Oh-so-even-faced, paramount, almost burlesque.

Hold still; you don't want to be a blur.
Face off your demons, count to ten and say
Cheese! Did you find the way out?

Even with that awful hangover, hold it
With both hands—sip, sip gently—with words
As soft as these one might just believe.

Hunger holds still, and then another
Will rise ashen from the Underworld with no more
Lone tears stepping out into the road.

All I'm saying is that it's a possibility.
Meanwhile, know that Death is the mistress
Of Art. Can you hear the bells calling?

Feathers of a Dead Turkey

Of Cargo

In autumn the wine is pressed; many
Toes give the fermentation a shine.

The ladies in their half-pinned buns,
The men harping on about their losses—

A paradise of tired eyes garrisoned
In the quarters in the form of exaltation;

But their faces are blank stone, etched
In some strange cratered version of the moon.

In winter, rewards are reaped for their
Foresight, visions of wild animals,

Lynxes and foxes, the rutting of the stag,
Even the extinct worlds of the mastodon,

Or the fire-eating wildebirds—the world
Replaced by a few bundles of twigs
Against the wall where the fire passed through.

But, in the evening, a ship at anchor awaits
This precious cargo of mythical tales.

Here the strange bins labeled seasonally
Know no hands or feet will linger,

The vexation of creation is neither
Closed in one landscape, nor at peace

In the rolling hills—everything is proportion,
Stepping ashore on an economy of passions;

These days are passed beyond expectations.
They who cast their fortune from afar,

Willed into the mechanics of the future.
A known thing, a dwelling from once before.

And know again that each season, wild
And fertile or stoic and bare, as it may be,

Recalls a memory—of flies upon flies,
Of a smattering of pollen and dust, of egg-

Laying insects in every form—and even when
Lucretius was blabbering, Amenicus was wandering,

Then Octavia in her flowing robes, Agrippina
Close to the edge, her hairpins and hair

Overflowing in daisies.

Savoir Faire

Let's move out at a snail's pace, tuck
Into time backward. Yes, there are
Logistical problems with this endeavor, but
On this, we need to stand alone, no one's
A single thing. Yes, I know that gives you
Pause. Whether one or two, what's the difference?
"The earth sends greetings." OK, so I assure you
It's all preserved in jam jars, in pickled beans,
In the million stairs you've walked
In your cascade of reality—no mind
What you think of reality—there are syn-
Aptic connections, all words written in lower
case. Let's feign
Admiration, then let's tear it to shreds
Inbetween the Turkish cigarette
And the absinthe. Yes, you fight back blindly,
But as well as any other couple, you use one um-
Brella, you embrace the cold and fog to-
Gether; one memory rides the wave, sees between
The fingers. It's not about our past,
You'll get no alms. I know it never occurred,
And yes, there is this sorrow, this faint
Buzz in the heart, as if all form is missing.
Who wouldn't be concerned. But some things
Can't be explained. What *is* our notion of existence?
The books, the pegs, the washing lines, the
Moss-hungry wrens building time for their own:
"She who perches all-reigning in the apple trees," or
"She who gasps away her own reality."
Don't gape. At the bottom of the basket,
Words aren't the least bit happy. Personally
I prefer to sleep on a modest blanket.

I Would Wager

A hundred thousand
Or two, a whisper
In your ear, or a flea;

A life story, seven
Dozen goose eggs;
And you, when you

Eye me at the bar
In all your confectionery,
Hold still. Let me see

The curls embroidered
In your mind—a hundred
Thousand or two,

A whatever on your lips,
The fringe of your
Feathers thinking

Nothing of themselves
But an image of time,
The curve of some earthly …

Oh, don't listen to me.
I barely read the papers.

Prelude to a Planet

Out here in the wastelands
Where industry broods,

A dark cloud of toxic fumes
Pours over the day.

Back in town, the earth
Is being dredged, exposing

The shiny shells of beetles,
Flies are burning up

Their flying machines
Seeking our dead meat,

Fragments of life that once were.
An army of empty, gleaming

Houses stands to attention,
Truth needs no furniture

They seem to say
With their glaring eyes,

As they hammer, the workmen
Clench their stained teeth.

Perhaps we'll meet again
In five hundred years

Somewhere in the swamps,
The deserted cemeteries,

Under crumbling bridges.
There we can dance

In a natural light, or walk
In the tracks of the bear

Along the river's narrow edge,
Tossing stones.

Arrowheads

Huddled in close, brow to brow,
The shells of our backs
Against the walls. Our breathing
Echoes as within a cathedral.

Later, lying, you say:
"You know each blood cell
Contains its own soul."

A cooling mischief settles.

Later still, sighing, you say:
"How does one get away with murder?
What century is this? What era?"

Outside, the towers wobble
From the planet's underbelly.

In a manicured garden beneath
The dome, a squirrel sits curved,
His blue eyes trained on the soil.

GDP

Everyday fact.
Ordinary.
Unaware,
Yet impossible.
The world's importance—
Where folks can kill with art—
At times because of dampness,
Inspiration; "love y'all when the light
Hits your eyes," when the light dies.
In the folds of your hands
Shakespeare always held up—
For a whole day, a year, more …
It depends. What no longer exists
Is unreliable. Dishes never seen
On disposable menus. Seriously.
But no, walk toward the economy,
Tie it up in you, weigh in.
Switch off the TV provided.
We don't know, but know you are
Always present where 3 roads meet.
Don't retreat. Send a few toads
Into their blessed solitude. Who
Would fail the great GDP?
"Not me," you say, "not me!"
Down in the Otherwise, where
Wise decisions are a tall order,
Where the could-be-great is really
Nothing at all. Be jolly,
Scatter yourself around, know how
In every procession great and small
There's some semblance of corruption.

The Coalition

Formally introduced. A motto.
Please refer to the administrative body.

There's a madman there
Who calls himself Mister Reform.

Let him be explained away—

"In history, that which descended
Upon the earth." What an entrance!

No refuse. Everything parceled and stamped.

And from the balcony, the children
Playing ball, the pitched tents

Under the dry fountainhead.
Swarms of bees. Don't ask.

It's a porcupine of a matter.
"Don't over-pet or over interpret!"

If we hadn't sped away
We could have picked up our own litter.

There's a madman here
Who call himself Mister Operator.

Turn of a Leaf

And, at this point of N-return, vessels
Crowded with imminent faces, the keen
Gray-blue green teeming with jellyfish.

Crows circling, gulls spitting out stones.
Pigeons picking up flakes of croissants—
Curious, this nation of wide-eyed dreams.

Then, like extras in a folk play,
That stepping ashore, that stroking
Of rough rocks—palms full of soil.

≈

Beyond the mighty fire-breathing butterfly,
Music, indelible music burning the air,
Yet coldly we settle into formation,

And we coldly move toward the desk
In this outpost of civilization, nodding
Si, Da Da, dui dui, Ja sicher …

And Ayyayai, give ourselves names like
Freedom and Destiny and Fate, like
Hope and Fate and Melody.

≈

And later than night, we stumble down
Alleys. "Yes, we see a land that stretches
Off into infinity," we sing. It goes on:

"And yes we can walk down to the mouth
Of the river talking prophecies and fortune
And favor, and let ourselves be swallowed whole."

Halogen Headlamp

Intelligentsia

Bold proposals fraught with intentions.
The burning of oil wells. Skies

Bathed in black. The transitory evidence
Scattering the air, but where the breath?

Congested in the thread of memory?
History as ashes or history as ashes and

Gold? Watch the molten puddle on the floor.
Have I become the flight of the beetle

Pressed into the sole of my shoe?

The blows keep coming from every angle.
A broader experience would suggest

An oncoming train—stark on the horizon
Where the trees give no shade—or a knife-

Edge-shunting between mounds of dirt,
A long line of children dancing.

The gesture flows into the winds.
Down upon the wharves again,

Where morning is moored.
Among the seaweed and the starfish.

A useless riddle.

A Golden Apple

A sad time for the old man—your portrait
Hanging over the mantel; across the threshold,

A passion for quiet words; how might that he
In his vagrant quarter, the neon quarter

Where prostitutes address their multitudes
In their garter and glitter, in their garb

And gab, in their fingernails and fluster.
"Would you look at that! Cat got your tongue?"

At the bench against the pitted wall I have found
All have departed as martyrs, something urges

Me to find a church and go inside, avoiding
The stare of gold, avoiding the supplicant

Saints and the pigeons fussing away. Yet,
The slow-blanched spires of the cathedral

Look far too divine, far too imposing.

At sunset, still on the bench observing the runes
In the clouds, attempting a smattering of

Old Norse; "By Zeus!" you say offering me a luke-
Warm coffee with those vacant eyes. "Let's off

To the Urals!" you cheer, pouring a hefty
Dose of irony. You tell me the story of a merchant

on his way to Harlem and a truck filled with canned goods
But with a mind to meet the Old Man in the Mountain.

You tell me of your time in a Trans-Siberian gulag,
Locked in the chains of the secret police.

Surely "Trans" means "moving," "ongoing," "at crossways."

Along the road to Nuovo Vitalis, you say,
Are to be found untold secrets. I feign away

For a second, for a minute or two. "Secrets
Like the Secret Police?" "Yes," you say,

"A pack of living beasts." But, my heart
Isn't in it as I turn to the Colonnade, watch

A woman sleeping in the shade, and feel the words
Of a great lama calibrating:

"If forty thieves on their way to Samsara
Might slip on the train tracks one after the other,

Or a trapeze artist burning high on drumbeats
Would fall at the sound of a kazoo, do you honestly

Think the Eiffel Tower will split in two
When an ice-cream van does the rounds?"

Morse Code

Arriving out of nowhere
As you are apt to do,
The city in a frantic

Turbulence, all but two
Faces, two masks etched
In forced smiles—

The wrinkles around
The eyes are a dead
Giveaway—the memory

Has no one to contain it.
I know you say it's all
Bread to me, and here's me

Breathing bad wine.
Dive deep into your
Catacomb of an office,

Weed out the morsels,
The old snapshots.
In war and peace

These things look
Alike, but try
I urge you, push

Your way through
The streets, across
The rusty bridge

And find your wings,
The law that speaks
Across the land, and

Know just where the arc
Of your eyebrow ends,
For the first time

In human history, flight
Seems like a lucky
Accident.

Limbic Spin

"Le bonheur des bon vivants," you said, thinking I would have no idea of what you spake. You said, "Les Legionnaires are a forgotten tribe who rose from the Kalahari." I said, "Remember, in those days we were content with a photo of the lake; yours in theirs." In those days, the conference had subsided, the candidates in their cryogenic crypts; all that churn-churning in the brain, slim pickings for the crows.

Repeat the phrase. Clearly things are not as you said (your exhalation, not mine). "Someday," you said, "you'll be without them too. Hope you can hope to achieve—between gratitude and fortitude (and by the way, it's all the rage)—and that eagerness, that circumnavigational route, the 'Lake that Would Not'."

Come on, it's early. Already the plumber is on vacation, and given his height, he will devour himself. Know this: I stand for you, you who belong amongst the rocks—and despite all the obstructions, that preponderance of envy, find the turtle, even without his maps—and likely a lack of decency (it ain't so heavy), his inventions are of his own making—despite your whines—know it will be impossible otherwise.

Memory from an Uneasy Armchair (or, No Feng Shui)

A flight of stairs moving upward,
Eagerly residential. The heavy
Suitcase in the hall, those

Unbelievably large eyes. Had
You worn that sweater before?
Admiration and pity in one burst.

Whatever's good for him is better
For me, or so the saying goes.
I remember the tone clearly.

Seeds cast in doubt, an homage
To the men in plaid pants and
Moccasins. Never renounce them,

Just know an abyss is an abyss,
A general theory of relativity—
Don't get too close. I want to

Laugh, but wherever you are,
Perhaps in the demarcation zone,
There's no substitute, not really,

Even a propensity for playing
Bridge. Is this the last time,
Or will there be another?

Hanging Out the Window for a Sparrow

Hunting in vain. There's blood on the boulder in front of the house, a herd of clouds have gathered in storm formation, and the spark that flared from the lightning bolt lifted our sparrow right out of his shoes. Your flight, driven from exile might pardon the stem of history, or perhaps in your luxuriant ways, even thought you may be betrothed, the fume of flowers has intoxicated you. It all reaches me in a minute—the heart of a heart, a wily thing draped in white cloth—everything is form. Dear Sparrow, the lights beyond the mirage; that which is transforming stutters, freezes; wait for no one, comb the sleepy wall, the ever-shrinking shade. What protrudes in its own sprawl may not be the bee-all. And, if you must, in fact think you rather should, throb in the crystal gaze of the thicket, know your destiny's conjoined with mine in a fate where the fittest survive; but Darwin's dead you say—and you're right; the hills slope away and the mosquitoes and no-see-ums as irritating and bothersome they may be, deliver the payload—for many years they lived in the verdant woods, upon the deer and the turkey—the spines on their faces high on clots and biometrics. Horizons too have been shaped by architects, each measure boundless in intention: a mirror? or an aftereffect? I leave this decision in your unlikely wings. You refuse the much, you say; don't reject the stem of the storm. Each passing whimsy is more, and swells the heart; across the fiber of your being, the shattered beam you have perched upon, know this: It rained on all of us, even you with your talons, even where the mad moth whirls or the wounded spring curls; in that festival of chills, the mouth of the siren's snow.

Has the Curse Been Dispelled?

Catching your gaze, the years
Of your youth unafraid, the age,
One of uncertainty. What will

Your grandchildren say of you?
So forgetful, poor teeth,
Your hands as common sense.

Not because lines are drawn
In the earth, more your sigh
Of relief. A primal cause, perhaps?

All these years alone that seemed
Like some never-ending Persian fable,
All that feasting upon eyes

Long before the taking-leave
Of the soul. Living, but never
Having lived, your youthful form

Now put to rest after the 2nd, no
3rd child. Do you remember the lover's
Rendezvous, the girl we saw dead

On a bed of rose petals? Hand on heart,
It's not easy to live without passion,
Practicing the art of elimination.

Surely champagne improves things,
Helps us swim in all the peopling.
Are lovers always fated?

Perhaps I'll save that for your gravestone.

Another Paradigm

In the age of statistics
Where the many are the more
And everything is multiplied

By mirrors, when we sus-
Pend belief in disbelief,
Even worldly illusion

Itself is a mirror.
We know the smokestacks
Are exploding even as

The picture implodes.
Time is enfutured in
The man arrested, the un-

Churched staring out,
The churched bending
The chains of history—

Leaving behind crypts,
Miniature chapels, end-
Less passageways and tunnels.

Birds of ill-omen
Circle the wreckage—
Of misanthropes, of

The deposed—if they ever
Existed or were penciled
In by the Minister of History

On his train journey home
Every weekday evening.

Styrofoam Barfly in a Bear Market

Lovers high in high grass, over tangled backs the sun storms down. The tower clock in town chimes even out here, and the constant heaving of the engines in the motorcycle works can be read about in the newspaper, that same paper where once we read about the sinking of the *Titanic*.

He wanted her to marry; he promised her a caravan and two hundred camels.

Every night he slept with her picture in eyeshot.

He dreamed them at the Pyramids smoking Gauloises unfiltered, the Saharan winds upon his back; but before they reached the desert, they stopped off for Cosmopolitans and a plate of lamb tagine and olives. That stop became night and then day, and then drunk they remained for three hundred miles, until, they reached an oasis and all around them across the horizon, people held up their arms as the stock market rose.

Bloody Tail of a Rabbit

Reading Signals Riding Surplus

My four uncles and three aunts have all made it through the Panama Canal, their childhood was upside down too, and then there's the wider effect. Their adventures have led them through pastel colors, contorting mirrors, exotic locales like the Dusty Wayward Minaret or the lumbering berth Teeside, just south of Newcastle upon Tyne; but on my coffee table, there's an old scrapbook replete with dinars, zlotys and the 100 Million Billion Pengo. Anything that's served at the Reliquary is well in hand, from the uniform button on the lapel in the shape of a wild boar to the Charles-Félicien Tissot pocket watch that served in World War One. You've saved the good furniture for this: Mother's lattice headrest and the best bread in the district. The rivalry is appalling. Who cares if Fuertaventura is in Spain or in Portugal or if one of our ancestors stuck up a stagecoach, who cares if you're a milk magnate or a jam baroness, or if that rifle bullet lodged in your head has still not killed you. Everything was inspired by a delegation of Oriental emissaries, but there's still something else: Having taken every liberty in the world, the leopard skin tacked to the barn door is just too much.

Murmurs

More than a year now, the strange crews work
Two by two as the airplanes drone overhead.

Ten plagues of Egypt have descended but even
Now to talk of them is strangely taboo.

Alligators raise their eyes to the surface
And the dome of the sky is the color of pumice.

Factory stacks are still puffing away—
All in the name of hard science. The scene opens

Like a newspaper, the landscape scarred in in-
Finite cracks, and just at this moment a traveler

Stands in the doorway. You can tell he has committed
A crime. His wry grin betrays any last chance

To meet the eyes. "Go on!" he cries, goading
The crews of two by two, to the prerogative of all.

"Sound words," he says. "Solid advice!" His ankle-
boots are sharkskin, his perfumed hat ripe

In a peacock plume, his sheen drenches the air.
"We knew it would come to this," he says pulling

three brand-new bills from his deerskin wallet.
"One of the most beautiful spots in North Oderphelia,"

He laughs. "We'll be finished in a week or two.
Then they'll all descend from the hills and flood

In here like a plague of rodents. Be ready," he says.
"They'll all try to fleece you." I nod quietly

Staring at the unfinished reinforced concrete.
A mouse crosses the street. A vulture circles.

Fallen Trees

for Miriam

Along the trail we come across
The tracks of a big, lumbering male,

Further still, tufts of dark fur
Snagged on a barbwire fence.

The sun beats down for an instant,
And suddenly we hear him rolling

In the mud, heaving and snorting.
The grass is high here, closing

Like a curtain on all forms beyond.
We thrive on imagination: an old vine

Becomes a venomous snake, a gnarled
Knot in a tree, the face of Grand-père.

The air chills, light is louvered
By clouds, a strange uneasiness

Like wanting to fall asleep in the morning.
A century ago and all those beautiful stories,

A hand within a hand of moist soil,
Moon rock, fertile as the crescent *lune*,

Long discussions and squabbles, a man's
Patent leather shoes covered in scat.

The first corn, the first pear trees
In bloom, the crows that followed us,

The glazed picture captured and framed.
See! They're cavorting: Time is not enough!

And yet, in a spasm of coughs, he appears,
That shaggy male, determined to hold on

To his mud, his own wild-crop, his own …
"Who's the plaintiff?" he roars, his teeth

Getting in the way. "Hold your ground," you say
Kicking me in the shin. We edge backward

To the edge of the precipice, a sheer drop
Said to be home to other more multifarious beasts.

Finally we stand in the cornfield, all alone
And still. Time and space, beginning and end

Fuse as one, and a little halo rises
Ever so gently over your skull.

Fallen Cities

for tt

In a dark fight with plastics: shopping
Bags, empty orange juice containers, coffee cup

Lids, and that constant tinkle of kicked up
Glass. Years of discarded reusables piled up

Then churned, half-digested and spat out, which
Gives the city its sheen, its acid flux

In the sweet vinegar of time, a layer of
Leisure, a capitulation that one fine day all will

Be dust, sand dunes, chalk or lime, either way
Fossilized. Where would we be without our accomplices?

Up ahead, down some forsaken alley,
The howling of dogs, the scurry of something,

Then a leap. Half-liquid-half-shadow
They flow through the city at night. Is this

A place? or a fragment of one? The stunning
Faces of those once here now gone creeps

Up on one. Wishing to find dreams alone,
To find the fountain at the end of the path,

The invented, the completely natural or super-
Natural. Here's a convenience store open late,

No, all night! A man frothing at the mouth
In the doorway, his head tilted skyward, but

No stars—staring deep into forever dark.
Lights in the windows raising the bar, man

Invented. The wintering of thought
Across the threshold of the shop, a single

Being transposed, and here, something better
Than light, the gold tooth of a cashier

From the heart of an exploding sun, a diamond
At its center, so that when hit by a flash

Of night, becomes a symbol of an ever-
Present Buddha. "Will you accompany her home?"

He asks me all smiles and packets of free matches.
"Of course," I say. And with your corndog

And Coke sipping loudly on a single straw,
You say: "There are only so many stars, and

They all follow the river." The moon appears
Through the smog, a bloodshot eyeball veiled

In ribbons of human thought. Below, a dead bird
Quivers, coming alive in large insects, their

Husks glowing against the eyeball. In this
Moment you want hope, genius! This is

The moment without a word, and you rear
Your graceful head, and like in a painting

By Renoir, you pixelate almost—what
Grace! And then, your meditation to an

Honest bloke. *"Rien, nada, nichts,"* you say
In that smoky way. Nevertheless, the sun

Is entering the picture and the heartbeats
I hear are not my own, but the sound of

A pickup truck nearing home. "Who will come,"
You say, "On that day you fly away?"

Cliffhanger

All hail the monster on this Hallow's Eve.
Watch the pandemonium unfurl, the damsel
In distress as the dull dawn rumbles.

A shadow stands watch over your grave.
Don't recoil from the long years of time, wait
Until day mushrooms into itself, know

The Way melds every living shadow, fills itself
Within us until we find our material self
In unison, at the top of the belfry with

The first rush of wings within the roots
Of the sun; let the voices boil up—first
Simmer on a low heat, gas is best, that assured

Flame in purple robes. Don't sob, we're
Perennials, Monster, and we know how to
Glow in the dark. Where do *you* lay *your* eggs?

Do you leap from branch to branch or crawl
Like the ivy? All the lashes to your frame—
A ladder among the clover? Be your full

Material self, press your face to mine.
Let me be a swallow to your hawk.
You've named a tree for me?

Cross the meadow and turn away from the stairs.
Are you still lying in waiting?
Don't fear the crowds in the street,

Return to your roots, your humble abode
Where hinges are rusty and voices
Barely audible. Recently, no wind arrived

With your premonition looking for you,
Scouting you out in the darkness. Me?
I still sink, but you, from the moment

Of your creation, encased in a shaft of light,
Not holy or risen, but brimming, over-
Flowing—a gift I dreamed in the high branches …

Meeting of the Town Council

The official map of this town lies in a safe in Old Man Edison's office. His is a club of patrimonial tribes knee-deep in martinis, stained walnut with brass fittings, and a powerful arc of history—nightly nightcaps by the fire, a panel of reindeer antlers, the curled horns of wild rams, an entire menagerie of rabbits, groundhogs and stuffed hares. Here's a bobcat pouncing midair, there's a miniature weasel snarling at the copper-coated wolf howling in situ. Up at the train station caskets are stacked up, oblong pine boxes marked "For Transport," in the dark hold of a foreign ocean vessel dancing on the fog in the North Atlantic. And the town and her villages lurking back between two marshy banks where waterfowl scare up into the sunset and tall chimneys line the pathways with promises of home. A hundred eyes flare up behind windowpanes at the wailing of a newborn or the bleating of bullfrogs, which abound in these parts. The ground quivers here, even under a blanket of snow, in the pine trees and the firs, in amongst the shrubs in Aunt Madeline's small garden where curious gnomes wear silver wings and the silhouette of some unknown creature crosses the train tracks in search of plastic containing the residue of yesterday's suppers.

Down at the creek, the minnows whisper: "Please let there be light."

In the Micro-Life of Oxygen

He who hears his infinite heart is someone
Who collapses brilliantly in his own star.
Someone who bears the burden, all those missed
Soccer goals—and by the way, the grass
Is never at rest. What luxurious hope to dwell
On this unshaken earth, the soil untilled.
The scared will flee, untethered; oh you
Pretend to flee, but only pieces float by
In an ocean of sky—something approaching
Astonishing. A callous hand admonishing
Something for her, for me, but you remain
Behind, on the edge of the oldest woodland,
Snagged on coral reefs, this portrait
Of you over the years, the rampart where
The cloud breaks, where the nimbus becomes
Cirrus, that ogle-eyed glare, the purpose
Of poetry; yes, the years in grass,
In carbon dioxide, in low-flying drones,
In the waste of me, in the unturning swivel,
That compact part of me in the unpronounced,
The passages of blood to the heart, the beat
Of a clock, that soiled part of me,
In the pure energy, little lightning strikes
One after two after one after three, in
The words as a way in, in the harmonious
Tread, the uncorked tree, the way my wake
Hovers over me, in that man-
Made part of me.

Riverfolk

The river seems to meet
Their eyes, staring back

Restlessly, a reckoning
That stuns all the nimble-

Footed villagers. The air
With its apathy for the with-

In or without, begins to tear
Them down to the foundations.

All that energy in the walls—
All the wires sprung loose

Beneath their feet—pouring
Away, their ancestors swept up

In a single breath, and the mud-
Bank bulging and stretching

Into a burning question.
On the third day, wrapped

In the sludge and fragments
Of old letters, a child gathers

Together a story of ancient
Monsoons, using words like

Destiny, horizon, happenstance.

Another, perhaps her cousin,
Fashions a broken branch

With a frayed electrical cord,
She crouches on the shore

And fishes for words like

Future, marriage, permanence.

Civilization

The shadow
Of the rain

Under the eaves
Of the barn,

Haze-filled
Spaces

Quivering in half-
Flickering light.

The ground becomes
Luminous; a ringing

Of fingers on tin,
And the mountain

Opens its windows.

Weeks pass.

Moths settle
On loose timbers.

Night comes slower.
A mystery rolls past.

Telegrams
From another world.

Existence

A handful of dry walnuts.

A balm for all wounds.

A snail's pace.

Two droplets of water.

No-territorial frontiers.

That which doesn't cross.

Memory without remembrance.

Innocence.

That blackbird pecking on the sill.

Religious objectives.

Righteousness. Gibberish.

The Event.

What's needed if you could make it without her.

What the tribe fails to observe tearing away from complexity.

Crumbs of honor.

A point where a word is *imperceptible*.

A border.

A halo of mist.

Frightening anthropomorphic gods.

Trial by fire.

Objects.

A gust of wind.

Native islands. All hearth.

Code.

Not touching the bottom.

One eye open.

Lessons taught
by marvelous destinies.

Control.

Something you can't say
despite your ears.

Everyday facts.

More code.

Camouflage.

More content than form.

Nipped in the bud.

Language and balance.

The rest is art.

Derangement / Backward

Perched like a miniature bird
On the mast of a sailboat

Deep in the ocean, awaiting
The coming storm—or far

Underground in a cavern
Of earth, where the sensation

Of height is that of a blind person;
Tapping the floor of this

Secret sanctuary, scattered
In old journal and diary

Entries, torn snippets
Of calmer weather, the traveling

Backward, the sense of debt
Is overwhelming—a rescued word

Springs forth to mark the limit;
Dwelling at the edge of the crater

Until nightfall, then morning,
And that search beneath a solid sky

For solidarity, for fair climes,
For reasonable passage, even if

Fate loses its force
And the storm is unveiled.

Meanwhile, On the Outskirts of Town

Through the trees, where few leaves
Hang on, names have been swallowed
By the cold. Cars streak by in a blur

Of abandon—and tell me, where are
The grasses and the flowers? The mingled
Notes of those huddled by the fire?

Straight out of the stratosphere
Thunder strikes a chord. Oh the restless
Shadows in my head—never before

Have I climbed through the window,
Wafted down to the waterfront
And let myself be blown about.

After a thousand years when you awaken
Will you know who you are? Or,
Will you imagine yourself

As a few minutes of fresh air
Streaming across a lake? Wouldn't it
Be wonderful to fall off a tree

Into a river and float on to great
Acclaim in the ocean. Consider
The things you would see drifting east.

The masses of water all collected
In one stiff drink. And the bridges
And the underpasses, the flood

Of light flowing through the reeds,
The seeds swirling on to new lands …

Here the seeds land on asphalt, and
Algae grows on dead men's beards.
Still, the chain of life pushes

On through the fog.
Turn over, sink six-feet-six.
Let the water wash over you.

Railroad Spike

Cast in Steel

All hands on deck,
The heaviness of the air

Predicts an evening of fog
From the other side.

In the eyes, out there
In the cold manifold

There is no belonging,
But here you are wishing

To draw from the source—Run!
The shattered ice

Of living waters, unbearable
To feel the darkness

Upon your face and
That flurry of vanished beings,

Of serpents and eels,
Of gargantuan man-eating squid,

Their fluid tentacles
upon your eyes, from

The seabeds running dry,
nothing foretold

On strong evidence
or strong existence, or

How the cosmic bird slowly
turns the earth, how

the seasons are all
the wisdom you'll ever get.

The *Saint Juliana* Rises

Juste les mots / les mots justes

The great unrest feeding you. Do not seek
The boundaries of the sea, the markers of passage;
Of salt, not smoke; of vigorous fish
In the cascade—a choice of obedience or insanity?

This summer, a single day vanished into
Its interior, an impetuous noon in abundant
Waters. If possible, watch your utterances
When the wave reaches its peak. Low
In the water, it's impossible to resist the decline,
The winged and the powerful deities in the sky,
The soft murmurs, a guessing game of
The absolute, perhaps the deepest secret of

All. The port window open on all this,
On the bounds and breadth, the quickening
And the deft, the flying fish migrating, the
Spray scattering apart in ashes in this hour of

Oil lamps and sea-lion courage, a dimension
In the making, advancing the structure of
Dawn, the sweet machinations of the anchor
In waiting until the mortal fire is passed through,

Then on into the mouth of the monsoon,
Into that nothingness which is everything,
That every moment repeating, every moment
Repeating, every moment repeating every moment:

A Break in Consciousness

In the basins of the Euphrates and the Tigris,
Identity was remaindered into the limitless

Deserts of Arabia, the mountain chains
Of Persia, tombs were hewn and raised to Horus

And Osiris, the bodies clad in their mummified
Rags, an assimilation of the Pharaoh's

Own voice, the admonitions of the lost,
The whispering of the waves, and finally,

The flood that came from but one mouth,
Just as the ancestors were cut from one cloth.

≈

Nothing but a few clouds now and across
The sands we ride—an act of love, no doubt.

How beautiful the silence, how after the last
Grain counted, the sky and earth lose

Their enchantment, and we reach the caravan's
Final stone, an etching carved beneath the surface.

Calling all lovers to invoke the stars,
To press forward in long, uneven strides.

≈

Even when the soul is aware of it, the heart
Speaks without a particle of error, then

The voices mingle, and what was so finely
Chiseled from the limestone, slate, diorite,

Standing in the seated rows of the tombs,
The offerings, the notion of a vital source,

The hieroglyphs of two arms uplifted
With flat outspread hands—something like will-

Power emerges, even when crossing these
Consuming sands at the end of a thousand

Detours, clairvoyance, and to my undying
Surprise here is no floor or ceiling. Further

Still, cut from all we resources we roll
Up into a ball of thought and build a tower.

≈

What, you ask, was its source? Why, the finger
That refuses the thimble, the king on the seat

Of his own father represented by a small
Humanoid bird, the pursued and the pursuing,

The hours that marry the gods.
       And so we climb

Deep into the tomb to keep watch, to keep
The riverbed flowing, even here,
                                    among the desert rats

And the whip-tailed scorpions, through a pinhole
We watch the redness of a single flower upon the sky.

A Brief Conversation with Consciousness

And how the origin, down
In the break where we
Dream and move forward

Is not about the departed
Or their famines, the epic
Goes on to talk of great gods

And their pestilences; here
The problem bursts open,
The epicenter begins what

Occurred in the illumination—
Bread, hard bread pulped
Into reconstitution, impass-

Ivity found a mind of its own,
The mentality that arises
From too much smoke;

The hashish person cannot
Therefore be trusted to fulfill
Their lot, that breaking up

Of swallows, the civilization
Of things backing into
Prosperity, preposterously.

Scandalous that indeed we
Are owned by different gods,
All wholly created, all

Exaggerated in that unit of
Social control and evictive
Evolution, a way that a police

State with more subscribers
Than citizens, one fist over
Another, wary of its reign,

Moves northward, toward
The open seas where crossings
Are fed with former inscriptions,

Where the collapse is redacted
And the people staring
At the end of a voice, at the

End of a vote, a probable
Creature of vice, then head
South-wind, embark land upon

Legend where intellect is
Subjective consciousness,
Where in the model of

Religion, a crisis is all
That is needed, where
The gods, earning their

Functions and their pro-
Portions simply vanished
Into distraction. Then

An upsurge where man alone
Faces that modicum, where
Theocracy induces a change

Of mind, a retaliation
Of conscriptions, a nascent
Symbol, a street to be

Walked beside, a head
To be seen, a feudal fetal
Position cherished, dis-

Cussed over reputable wines,
Over the forsaken fallen,
Over the founding fathers,

Over this sparkling new city,
Over the Rome-in-a-day,
The hierarchy, the weary

And disturbed, the logic
Such that the idea of evil
Is where gods live, where

That other face, that some-
Times senseless passage
Is another's. It is said,

If a horse enters a home
Then that household will be
Scattered. It is known.

Here lies an empty window.

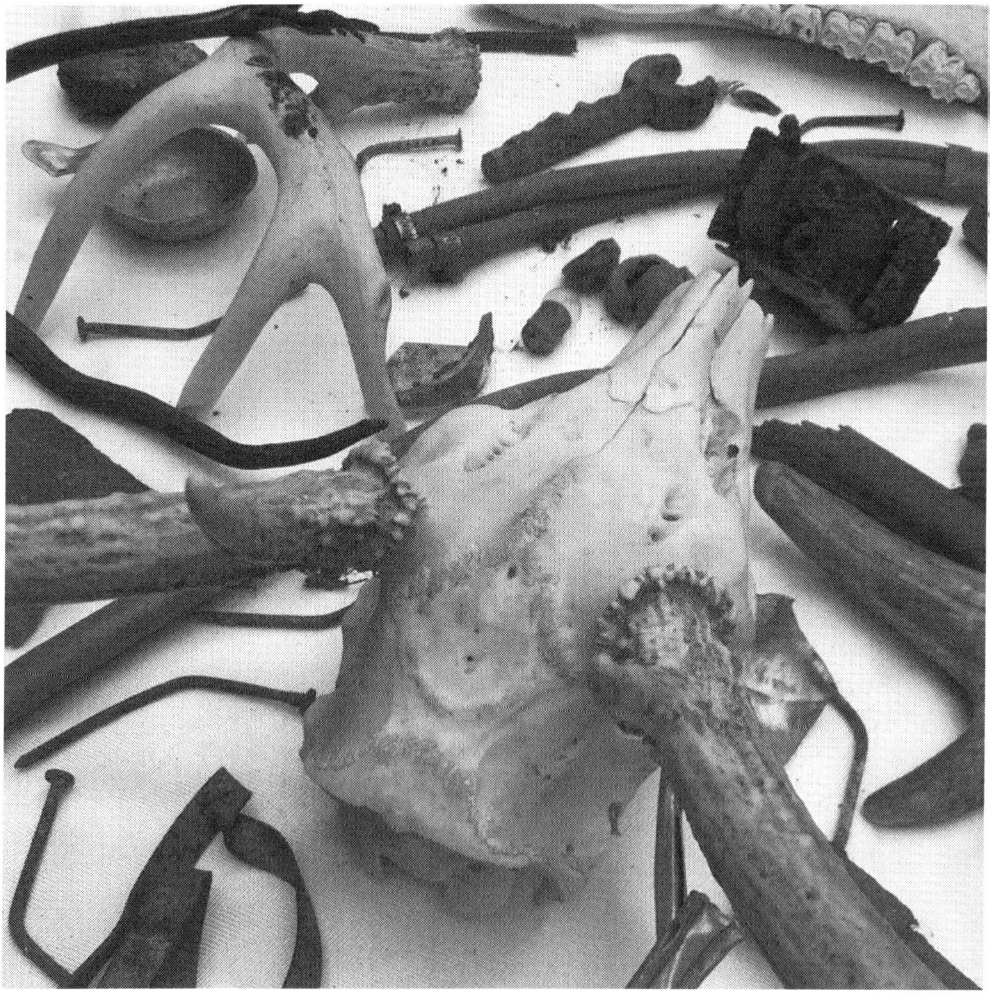

One More for the Road

In this last one thing let us not fail our forebears. No more pussyfooting around. Let us head straight for the light.

"But hold on! Isn't that a moth to a flame," you say, lighting up that sweet ganja on the way to the market square, a place where all we creatures forage under the eaves.

Old Man Tabernacle reminds you that anything you say will be taken into evidence. He grinds himself up like an organ when he needs to.

Emerge, Sweet Creature, and light up the way.

A Few Afterthoughts

Reflections on Marc Vincenz
by Robert Archambeau

Where a Poem Begins

"A poem may arise," Marc Vincenz once told Tom Bradley, "with a visualization; or it may make itself known sonically through an opening line, a mental image or a melody that leads the rest of the poem musically or imagistically." His comment is a good tip for the reader approaching the poems gathered here. Vincenz's poems have many of the markers of the anecdote-based lyric—a first person speaker, a setting, sometimes a second-person addressee, and even, on occasion, something like a moral to be drawn ("reserve/Absolute judgment," say). They have everything, one might say, but the anecdote. This is not to be lamented: indeed, at a time when most poems still depend on incident and story, Vincenz's writing feels refreshing. His avoidance of straightforward anecdotes comes from his sense that the poem must generate itself not from a lyric response to a single external event, but from its own internal logic: from a sound or an image that leads to another, related sound or image. "From time to time," he says in his interview with Bradley, "there are themes or images that arise in those semi-conscious moments that drive the narrative along its *axis mundi* (or axiom).... The journey itself then becomes the network or web that links these islets into a Oneness.... Only after the journey can the map be drawn and charted." A poem, then, is less a sensitive response to an established or known event, but a groping after what can be found in a series of related elements as they unfold.

Consider the six sections of "Something Like Courage." The first section speaks of "absolute objects," and the second picks up on the word "object" to introduce ideas of subjectivity and objectivity. Along the way, the second section touches on the idea of flight. Vincenz follows up on this seemingly incidental mention to speak of "insects winging toward day" in the third section, flying bullets in the fourth section, and a small, plucky "Chaplinesque bird" in the penultimate section. Ideas connected to this bird develop in the final section, which ends with the conclusion "I think I've finally discovered my wings." There's a journey, here—a pattern of development—but it's associative, not narrative or, strictly speaking, meditative. Vincenz trusts in the associative power of the poem's parts the way a Tarot card reader trusts in the cards dealt out in patterns from the deck.

A poem that begins with semi-conscious themes or images and develops through association can hint at narrative, as many of Vincenz's poems do—but consistency or completion is hardly the point. In this sense, Vincenz's work is like that of the Elliptical poets famously described by Stephanie Burt as setting out to write poems that "manifest a person-who speaks the poem and reflects the poet-while using all the verbal gizmos developed over the last few decades to undermine the coherence of speaking selves." Elliptical poems, like Vincenz's, "tell almost-stories, or almost-obscured ones."

Where a Poem Takes Place

Sometimes, in a Marc Vincenz poem, we know exactly where we are. We couldn't be much more specifically located, for example, than we are at the beginning of "A Few Thoughts": "The views from the bridges, high above the Taj Mahal, the deserts of northern India, the shining pools and dense scrub, the rapids and the trains." But then something like this happens:

> Suddenly there was a flash of light and the suitcase was crawling with insects. A small tree was at its center, and growing beside, thousands of mushrooms: chanterelles, polypores and morels, the Penny Bun and the Hen of the Woods, the Lobster and the Jack-o'-Lantern.

We're not in Agra, India, anymore. Even if we allowed for the marvels of a tree suddenly growing from a suitcase, those various mushrooms are not native to any single environment, and some don't appear in India at all. Wherever we are, it can't be found on any conventional map.

Often Vincenz drops us in a location that, while tremendously specific, could also be almost anywhere in the 21st century's globalized economy: a 24-hour convenience store, say, whose clerk speaks a different version of the English language than we do. Or we may find ourselves dockside someplace where:

> The ferryboat smells of something approximating
> Sulfur and crude oil. We stand on the jetty.
> There's a gentle knocking as if the Earth
> Were trying to hold still. Frayed plastic bags
> Float in the dockyards. I can read a few:
> *Bonus, Max Best, Indran's Dollar Emporium,*
> *Cash Corner, Sanigore's Choicest Cheapest.*

The shop names on the bags are tremendously specific, tied as they are to the micro-geography of individual small businesses. But they could also be floating in the trash-filled waters of almost any port on earth. One way to think of this is as Vincenz's comment on the collapse of geographic distance in the era of advanced capitalism. Another way to think of Vincenz's places, though, is as a kind of assemblage—fragments of real places spliced together with parts of other places, real or imagined, seen on a map or drawn from the depths of dreams. "Mythical lands," Vincenz has called them, "or lands of the wandering mind, if you will. These mythical lands are assemblages of many cultures.... These are reflections of many eyes and tongues, many senses—real or imagined."

Vincenz is a wanderer or nomad of sorts—his background Swiss and English via Hong Kong, Iceland, and North Carolina, his native languages many, his culture and family history hybrid and varied. Sometimes, then, it's hard to say when a passage grows from external experience or when it grows from the kingdom of dreams. "Reading Signals Riding Surplus," for example, begins this way:

> My four uncles and three aunts have all made it through the Panama Canal, their childhood was upside down too, and then there's the wider effect. Their adventures have led them through pastel colors, contorting mirrors, exotic locales like the Dusty Wayward Minaret or the lumbering berth Teeside, just south of Newcastle upon Tyne; but on my coffee table, there's an old scrapbook replete with dinars, zlotys and the 100 Million Billion Pengo.

It seems like fantasy, but with Vincenz, one can't quite be sure.

In the end, though, it doesn't much matter whether the geography is consistent with the external world or the realm of dreams, because Vincenz's geography is consistent with itself. His world, whether in these poems or in books like *This Wasted Land* or *Becoming the Sound of Bees* is always a despoiled one, replete with money-hustlers and environmental disasters. It is a world that weighs on its inhabitants, who yearn for some escape, for some place (real or otherwise) that lies outside the reality they know. In the creation of a landscape both geographically inconsistent and personally specific, Vincenz is like the young Auden (with his lead mines and feuding families among the hills) or, to turn to a poet more closely associated with Vincenz, like Ben Mazer (with his film sets from old Hollywood and his decadent wealthy families by the rolling sea). Someday, if someone writes a study about poets of geographic fantasia, Vincenz will merit some pages there.

Surely Some Revelation Is at Hand

Someone's always dreaming of vast profits—
From the mineshafts of the Transvaal
To the sandstone quarries of Szechuan
Each of them digging deeper into forgetfulness.

These lines from Vincenz's poem "Inedible" don't just give us his typical, despoiled landscape. They show us humanity lost in the pursuit of profit to the extent that we've forgotten—well, what exactly? Something for which the antithesis is profit and environmental destruction, surely. But can we say more than that?

It's easier to claim that Vincenz sees the visible world as fallen than it is to say what he sees as redemptive. In "Another Paradigm," he writes that we live in "worldly illusion," an unreal reality conditioned by those in power, where even the deposed leaders of old regimes may have been "penciled in by the Minister of History." In this world we find many characters waiting for vision, standing "on the edge of absolution" as they wait for "that fateful moment of self-discovery," as Vincenz puts it in "Facial Mud Scrub." It is a world where we are pulled toward something invisible, something that promises redemption, revelation, vision, perhaps salvation.

We are always at a threshold, in Vincenz's poems— at a border beyond which we sense a possible, tantalizing enlightenment. Sometimes we catch a brief flash of satori in the unlikeliest of places: the gold tooth of a cashier, for example, catches the light and becomes "a symbol of an ever- / Present Buddha." Sometimes the Great Truth seems more constant, though it nevertheless eludes our grasp. These stanzas from near the conclusion of "Inorganic Roots on a Deserted Island" put us in just such a situation:

> And so I climb the cliffs just as you
> Suggested and inch my way toward the crux.
> Bitter blindness descends as I rise, a vapor
>
> Of thought swirls above my head.
> At the peak a stork leans into the sky.
> Beyond the clouds, undeviated flight.

One might think of Shelley's "Mont Blanc," here: a mountain whose peak represents an enlightenment as sublime as it is inaccessible. Thought, it seems, stands between us and revelation. It is fitting, then, that instead of a doctrine, the poem gives us an image—the stork's flight, imagined on the other side of the clouds.

Jung once argued that the poet who works intuitively—not to illustrate an existing idea but to follow an impulse and let that urge find its shape—would give us poems that are inherently hard to pin down. In them, he claimed, we would expect:

> ... a strangeness of form and content, thoughts that can only be apprehended intuitively, a language pregnant with meanings, and images that are true symbols because they are the best possible expressions for something unknown—bridges thrown out towards an unseen shore.

Marc Vincenz works in just the manner Jung describes, and produces poems that can best be approached in the spirit of openness and exploration. Think of them as bridges, and let me know what you find on the other shore.

On the Poetics of Marc Vincenz
by Philip Nikolayev

I have closely followed the poetry of Marc Vincenz for roughly seven years now. He is a robust and energetic contributor to postmodern poetics, and one of those avant-garde poets who, although dissatisfied with the traditional forms of lyric verse, ensure in their best work that postmodern poetry retains a human face, a human touch, and an element of old-school, undeconstructed vividness.

While the idea of experimentation was optimistically borrowed by twentieth-century literature from science, "experimental poetry" is a misnomer because it includes no criterion of verification for judging the success or failure of an experiment. Typically, a perceived success or failure is a matter of preconceived opinion, of faith. The mere correspondence of an experimental work to some clever overarching literary theory does not constitute a valid criterion of success. On the contrary, the experiment—to be worthy of the name—must help verify or falsify the theory. However, this never happens anymore. The outcomes of avant-garde experimentation are unverifiable, they are simply "there." Hence, the avant garde's ethos tends to be self-congratulatory: experimentation goes by the enthusiastic euphemism of "innovation" and all putative poetic experiments are always deemed a success within the milieu that generates them. It is hard to find in postmodern literature a hard and sober look at its own failed experiments: this could be some new avant-garde critic's claim to greatness. Now that the era of literary theory has passed, poetic experimentation has on the whole become a diffuse and directionless affair.

In my opinion, Vincenz's poetry stands out happily against this rather dry background. It must be noted that Vincenz is not a theorist, but a practitioner. His writing is guided by the highly developed intuitions of a sophisticated poet, but in each case these intuitions are specific to the poem, not to some overarching theory. Nor is he or has he ever been an academic, and he has written precious little literary criticism. He is unmistakably highbrow, but in a different sort of way. Although his poetry relies amply on his free-wheeling imagination, it could not have arisen without his intense and geographically diverse real-life experience. Born in the '60s in Hong Kong's Matilda International Hospital to Anglo-Swiss parents, Vincenz grew up all over this globe. He has lived in China, Hong Kong, Iceland, Spain, Switzerland, the UK, and the U.S. He speaks several languages fluently and has traveled the world far and wide, from the grass plains of Mongolia to the mountains of Romania to the jungles of Brazil. He has worked as a designer, musician, craftsman, inventor, journalist, administrator, and chef. He now resides on a rural farm in the Berkshires, Massachusetts, where there are more opossums, black bears and raccoons than there are people.

Vincenz is literally a man who has seen a great deal in his life, and, not coincidentally, one always finds a strong visual flow in his poetry. The avant-garde movie of his verse alternates between the fixed, disillusioned and objective stare of the lens and moments of subjective implosion, when the camera goes dancing around, intermittently trying to peer into itself. Apart from the obvious merry bag of literary devices, it may be useful, in reading Vincenz, to think of such film-editing techniques as montage (sequencing a series of brief shots to condense space, time, and information) and collage (juxtaposing found footage from disparate sources).

I would like to offer my reading of Vincenz's poem "Something Like Courage" to illustrate the argument above and to give a good taste of how this poet's poetry works. The poem stands as a personal manifesto. We should note here parenthetically that an avant garde depends on its grand manifestos, which are often its most energetic and engaging texts, as distinct from its poems. ("Theories are much more interesting than poems," the Russian "language poet" Arkadi Dragomoshchenko once told me, and I get an exactly similar sense from the American academic avant garde.) By contrast, it is a strength of Marc's that he embeds personal micro-manifestos and aesthetic principles directly into his poetry, into the redeeming context of the poems themselves. I find this to be, in his case, a highly effective technique. It gives useful clues as to how the poet himself understands his texts, and it organically embeds his aesthetic declarations into the body of the work. The "theoretical" or at any rate broadly abstract elements are presented up front, in-your-face—as the first principles of a given text—and are kept mercifully brief, as if intimating, "These are the aesthetic concerns behind this poem" (and, by plausible extension, of these poems). Such is this work's "metapoetic," self-referential aspect.

I treat "Something Like Courage" (attend to the skeptical, Ashburyesque note that the title strikes) as a poem rather than a sequence, but the distinction is immaterial so long as we realize that it works as a whole, developing kaleidoscopically from a declaration of aesthetic principles toward a lyric resolution. Each of the six sections is in the shape of a verse paragraph of several lines followed by a single separate concluding line. The work begins:

> Find a storm, find resolve, draw
> On its raw quality; express free
> From absolute objects, reserve
>
> Absolute judgment.

This is at once the poet's self-motivation, with a reminder on how to go about the business of imaginative creation, and a clue to the reader as to how make sense of the text. The energy of creation flows from discovering the wild tempestuousness of life ("find a storm") and feeds on its primal energies ("its raw quality"), achieving an indeterminate, non-deterministic vision liberated from concrete imagery and sense ("absolute objects"), such that we cannot know immediately what to make of it: we must "reserve" a decided opinion ("absolute judgment"); i.e., delay it while also, by implication, reserving our eventual right to it. In other words, dare and see what happens.

Section 2 of the poem, whose ideas follow of a fashion upon those of section 1, "deconstructs" (for lack of a more attractive word) the old rationalist dichotomy between the objective and the subjective.

> Right of the object, objectively sub-
> Jective (not part of the poem's ob-
> Jective, more acutely [full of rights], full
> Of lights. Oh yes, an old man on a merry-go-round!),
> Agile flight—vibrant, ringed in gold
> And umber, sun-soaked like an effervescent
> Chemical reaction or some illicit form of transport.
>
> A variable species.

Here, the poem engages in the constant push and pull between the inseparable poles of objectivity and subjectivity. The point seems to be that the subject of an experience is always also the object of that experience. The anxiety of subjectivity, of subjectivism, is overcome here by embracing subjectivity's poetic inevitability. The words "subjective" and "objective" differ chiefly by the phoneme [s], since "sub-" and "ob-" rhyme closely enough (at least in American English). The first two lines of this section use line-end hyphenation to split the adjectives "objective" and "subjective," in each case enjambing the morphological root away from the prefix to create the *sub-/ob-* rhyme. This illustrates that the two implied extremes—naïve realism on the one hand and utter solipsism on the other— are barely if at all distinguishable, basically the same. Things are in flux between the two poles. Therefore, any experience, including aesthetic perception itself, is "objectively sub- / jective." The verse illustrates this effectively in vivid lines that produce a kind of synesthesia of these two fundamental aspects of experience or perception. The evocative phrase "an old man on a merry-go-round!" seemingly describes an "absolute object"; however, it automatically produces a particular feeling, a subjective sensation that we gain by empathizing, as is our nature as readers, with an old man so oddly positioned, and we visualize the whole merry-go-round full of children, a cheery tune playing as it spins: an existential, lyric moment. Everywhere in Vincenz, elements of objective and subjective diction are juxtaposed and intertwined. Life itself, come to think of it, is a "sun-soaked ... effervescent / Chemical reaction."

In section 3 of the poem we move from philosophizing to the concrete experience, disarmingly unassuming and universally familiar, of being stung by insects.

> Insects winging toward day, not taut
> Or pretentious, excessively sensitive—
> And, Dear Creature, stinging. (I mean no offense.)
> A forever burrowing into subterranean airports.
>
> Mostly offensive less offending.

We first see and hear insects "winging toward day"—an intentionally chosen poetic cliché—but the expectation of finding traditionally descriptive nature poetry is disrupted with the "not … / …pretentious" carnal stings of no-see-ums that forever churn out of their "subterranean airports" (presumably though not necessarily a metaphor of insect dwellings, from which they launch their inoffensive offensives to get our blood). We briefly feel the innocent (objectively "offensive" yet not subjectively "offending") sting of the real.

Section 4 possibly does not mean anything definite or defensible. This may be so because the indeterminacy of meaning is a part of these texts' message. The alternative possibility is that indeterminacy is merely a decoration or special-effect fog for the more lucid part of the text, for the somewhat determinate and determinable overall sense that this poem makes. There is no way to untangle the "subjective/objective" riddle of such a postmodern text except by sticking with a kind of daring, a leap of poetic faith, or at any rate a suspension of disbelief in the powers of the speaking self that is obsessed with subverting the conventional reflexes of textual and experiential coherence. Life can be incoherent and fuzzy, and the poem conveys this.

> As if we had been stray bullets, or indeed,
> Pieces of buckshot, as if the side-
> Walk cafes and their steaming frappuccinos,
> As if all the Frenchmen in the world might
> Play the fiddle.
>
> Easy to say: et cetera et cetera.

I like for its own sake the beautifully dramatic opening—"As if we had been stray bullets"—suggestive of the human condition, of our lack of free will. One thing I will say for this poet is that he has many well-turned, crisp, memorable lines that leap out at the reader and justify the reading process. In "Something Like Courage," every segment contains such lines. But instead of all the other possible directions in which this fourth part of the poem could have developed from this suspenseful starting point, perhaps parodically, "we" turn from bullets into buckshot, then into frappuccinos, and eventually info fiddling Frenchmen (*mais pourquoi, Monsieur?!*), "et cetera et cetera." Here, we are not supposed to care why: not all riddles are of such form as to invite a solution.

In part 5 of the poem we meet an intriguing character, an anthropomorphic avian:

> Let us find a consonant without easy listening,
> With a full wingspan, and to our surprise
> This extremely small, slightly resistant
> Sparrow—more than a tramp—a kind Chaplinesque bird,
> But particularly this sparrow, a bundle
> Of good intention, holds its head well.

An opening gambit.

The "consonant without easy listening, / [but] With a full wingspan" is a metonymic image of a baby sparrow, already hopping about, symbolic of birth and new life. (Feel free to YouTube baby sparrows chirping for their mothers to verify that they pretty much sound all consonant and no vowel.) This segment of the poem is unmitigated, optimistic lyricism. The lovely characterization "This extremely small, slightly resistant / Sparrow" (where a cliché-monger would have written "tiny, fragile") is suddenly morphed by juxtaposition with the great comedian of silent cinema: "more than a tramp—a kind Chaplinesque bird." We suddenly feel the exciting promise of merriment and adventure in the well-intentioned bird child's "opening gambit" on this earth. Just like any child's, we might add. If I am not mistaken, the ability to hold the head well is desirable in both bird and human babies.

In the concluding part 6, the bird has grown up to become the poet, now writing at the height of his powers: the camera's focus turns upon the first-person speaker himself. With "something like courage," as the title anticipated, the speaker informs the world of his poetic self-evaluation:

> I have written several masterpieces
> With several tragic actors. Let's call it
> "Estimated," let's call it "unfledged."
> Concerning the matter of the rereading, well
> It all has to do with balance and flight,
> Not the progress of science: what we want
> To describe—a process of nothing—the quality
> Of each thing and a recompense on canvas.

I think I've finally discovered my wings.

"I have written several masterpieces," yet I am still "unfledged," "[under-]Estimated," i.e., sheer potential in process of self-realization: have we not all felt like this at one point or another?

Vincenz came to systematic verse writing late in his career as a human bird of passage, yet his alighting upon the literary scene has been confident, prolific, and compelling. The author of 18 poetry books and 10 collections of poetic translation, and editor of MadHat Press, Vincenz is a formidable presence in the poetry world. He has achieved "balance and flight"— "flight" perhaps with a sense of his convoluted geographic peregrinations (that would be the envy of any single bird, with the possible exception of the pirate's parrot), culminating in his settlement in a time zone a full 12 hours behind the one into which he was born—but also definitely "flight" as the meditative flow of inspiration. This poet's aesthetic goal, summed up as "To describe—a process of nothing—the quality / Of each thing and a recompense on canvas," buddhistically eliminates the nothing/everything dichotomy. "I think I've finally discovered my wings" is a feeling that many of us know and will recognize.

We should appreciate how satisfyingly this kaleidoscopic and partially opaque poem clicks into focus in its conclusion. The whole work turns out to have been the poet's meditation on aspects of experience and on his flight (by means of "some illicit form of transport") into poetry, into being a poet. This mini-manifesto—this affirmation of literary self-worth—eclectically and eccentrically combines philosophical and aesthetic discourse with observations about insects and birds and other chitchat, yet eventually all this resolves, propelled by the contrastive energies sparked along the way, to a mighty personal lyric chord.

    I delight in experimental verse that, instead of deconstructing old-fashioned values and traditional standards of poetic quality, successfully honors them and meets their challenge, while also at the same time doing something wild. As elsewhere in the poetry of Marc Vincenz, the experiment succeeds here by the criteria of vividness and memorability.

Acknowledgments

"Prelude to a Planet" appeared in *The American Journal of Poetry*.

"Of Cargo" appeared in *Boston Compass*

"An Underpass," "Inedible," and "Here's Something Totally Unexpected" appeared in *LiVE MAG!*

"Something Like Courage," "Inedible," "A Dozen or So," "Inorganic Roots on a Deserted Island," "A Few Thoughts," "All Thumbs," "Facial Mud Scrub," "Limbic Spin," "Another Paradigm," "Reading Signals Riding Surplus," "Murmurs," "Fallen Cities," and "Meeting of the Town Council," appeared in *spoKe*

"On the Poetics of Marc Vincenz" by Philip Nikolayev and "Reflections on Marc Vincenz" by Robert Archambeau originally appeared in *spoKe*

Many thanks to Jonathan Penton, *Unlikely Stories* and Unlikely Books for all the friendship and support over the years.

About the Author

Marc Vincenz is an Anglo-Swiss-American poet, a fiction writer, translator, editor, publisher, designer, multi-genre artist and musician. He has published sixteen books of poetry, including more recently, *Leaning into the Infinite, The Syndicate of Water & Light, Here Comes the Nightdust, Einstein Fledermaus* and *The Little Book of Earthly Delights*. An album of music, ambients and verse, *Left Hand Clapping*, is forthcoming from TreeTorn Records. Vincenz is also a prolific translator and has translated from the German, Romanian and French. He has published ten books of translations, most recently *Unexpected Development* by award-winning Swiss poet and novelist Klaus Merz (White Pine, 2018) and which was a finalist for the 2016 Cliff Becker Book Prize in Translation. His translation of Klaus Merz's selected poems, *An Audible Blue*, is forthcoming from White Pine Press. Vincenz is editor and publisher of MadHat Press, and publisher of *New American Writing*. He has lived all over the world—from Spain to China to Iceland to India. He was born in Matilda Hospital on the Peak in Hong Kong, but now lives on a farm in rural Western Massachusetts overlooking Herman Melville's Greylock Mountain with his family and their Australian Cobberdog, Emily "Miloush" Dickinson. Portrait by Sophia Santos.

Other Titles by Marc Vincenz

POETRY

The Propaganda Factory, or Speaking of Trees
Mao's Mole
Gods of a Ransacked Century
Behind the Wall at the Sugarworks
Beautiful Rush
Additional Breathing Exercises (Bilingual: German-English)
The Wasted Land: and Its Chymical Illuminations (annotated by Tom Bradley)
Becoming the Sound of Bees
Sibylline (illustrated by Dennis Paul Williams)
The Syndicate of Water & Light
Leaning Into the Infinite
Here Comes the Nightdust
Einstein Fledermaus
The Pearl Diver of Irunmani
The Little Book of Earthly Delights
There Might Be a Moon or a Dog

LIMITED EDITIONS AND CHAPBOOKS

Benny and the Scottish Blues (illustrated by Dareen Dewan)
Genetic Fires
Upholding Half the Sky
Pull of the Gravitons

TRANSLATIONS

Kissing Nests by Werner Lutz
Nightshift / An Area of Shadows by Erica Burkhart and Ernst Halter
A Late Recognition of the Signs by Erica Burkhart
Grass Grows Inward by Andreas Neeser
Out of the Dust by Klaus Merz
Secret Letter by Erica Burkhart
Lifelong Bird Migration by Jürg Amman
Unexpected Development by Klaus Merz
Casting a Spell in Spring by Alexander Xaver Gwerder
An Audible Blue: Selected Poems by Klaus Merz

FICTION

Three Taos of T'ao, or How to Catch a Fortuitous Elephant

Recent Titles from Unlikely Books

~getting away with everything
by Vincent A. Cellucci and Christopher Shipman
fata morgana by Joel Chace
Typescenes by Rodney A. Brown
Political AF: A Rage Collection by Tara Campbell
The Deepest Part of Dark by Anne Elezabeth Pluto
Swimming Home by Kayla Rodney
Manything by dan raphael
Citizen Relent by Jeff Weddle
The Mercy of Traffic by Wendy Taylor Carlisle
Cantos Poesia by David E. Matthews
Left Hand Dharma: New and Selected Poems
by Belinda Subraman
Apocalyptics by C. Derick Varn
Pachuco Skull with Sombrero: Los Angeles, 1970
by Lawrence Welsh
Monolith by Anne McMillen (Second Edition)
When Red Blood Cells Leak by Anne McMillen
(Second Edition)
My Hands Were Clean by Tom Bradley (Second Edition)
anonymous gun. by Kurtice Kucheman (Second Edition)
Soy solo palabras but wish to be a city by Leon De la Rósa,
illustrated by Gui.ra.ga7 (Second Edition)
Blue Rooms, Black Holes, White Light by Belinda Subraman
Scorpions by Joel Chace
brain : storm by Michelle Greenblatt (Second Edition)
Ghazals 1-59 and Other Poems
by Sheila E. Murphy and Michelle Greenblatt

Made in the USA
Middletown, DE
02 November 2022